Muslim Festivals
Through the Year

Anita Ganeri

W
FRANKLIN WATTS
LONDON•SYDNEY

This edition 2007

First published in 2003 by Franklin Watts

Copyright © Franklin Watts 2003

Franklin Watts
338 Euston Road
London NW1 3BH

Franklin Watts Australia
Hachette Children's Books
Level 17/207 Kent Street
Sydney, NSW 2000

A CIP catalogue record for this book is available
from the British Library

Dewey number 297.3'6

ISBN 978 0 7496 7362 8

Printed in China

Franklin Watts is a division of Hachette Children's Books.

Editor: Kate Banham
Art Direction: Jonathan Hair
Illustrations: Peter Bull
Educational Consultant: Alan Brown
Faith Consultant: Usamah Ward, Muslim Educational Trust

Designer: Joelle Wheelwright
Picture Research: Diana Morris
Map (p26): Aziz Khan

Picture Credits:
Britstock-IFA: front cover; C & D Hill/Andes Press Agency: 20t; Christine Osborne
Pictures: 6t, 7, 8, 11b, 12t, 12c, 14, 15b, 16t, 16b, 17, 21b, 22t, 23t, 24;
Franklin Watts Photo Library: 9 all, 18t, 19b, 25b, 27b Steve Shott; © Trip: 6b, 10,
11t, 13, 15t, 18, 21, 25t, 27t.

Whilst every attempt has been made to clear copyright, should there be any
inadvertent omission please apply in the first instance to the publisher regarding
rectification.

Contents

Words printed in **bold** are explained in the glossary.

Introduction

Muslims are people who follow the religion of Islam. Muslims believe in one God, called Allah. They believe that Allah created the world, and sees and knows everything. In the **Arabic** language, the word 'Islam' means 'obedience'. Muslims obey Allah's will and follow Allah's guidance in their lives.

Muslims worship at a ***mosque***. *They take off their shoes before they go inside.*

Muslim beliefs

Muslims believe that Allah sent messengers, called **prophets**, to teach people how to live a good life. The last and greatest of the prophets was a man called Muhammad. He was born in the city of Makkah, in the country we now call Saudi Arabia, in 570CE. The Prophet Muhammad received many messages from Allah which he taught to the people around him. These messages were later collected as the **Holy Qur'an**, the Muslims' sacred book. To show respect, Muslims often write the letters 'pbuh', or the Arabic sign ﷺ after the prophets' names. These stand for the words 'Peace and blessings of Allah upon him'.

Modern-day Makkah, in Saudi Arabia, is a busy city.

Islam spreads

After the death of Muhammad in 632CE, Islam spread from Saudi Arabia to North Africa, the Middle East and Spain. Today, there are about 1,000 million Muslims living all over the world, and Islam is the world's fastest-growing religion. The two main groups of Muslims are the *Sunnis* and *Shi'ahs* (see page 11).

Muslim festivals

The two most important festivals in Islam are *Id-ul-Fitr* (see page 20) and *Id-ul-Adha* (see page 24). The word 'Id' means 'feast' or 'celebration'. In Muslim countries, these are public holidays, when Muslims celebrate and thank Allah. But there are many other special occasions during the year, when Muslims remember the life of Muhammad and events in their religion's history.

Many children dress up for the festival of Id-ul-Adha. This young Pakistani girl is dressed as a bride.

Festival dates

Islam uses a calendar which is based on the moon. Each of the 12 months begins when the new moon is seen. A moon month is about 29 or 30 days long, giving a shorter year than the everyday Western calendar. Each year, the Muslim months start earlier than the year before. This means that, from year to year, festivals fall at different times of the year in the everyday calendar. (See page 28 for the names of the Islamic months.)

Friday Prayers

The Holy Qur'an tells Muslims to pray five times a day – at daybreak, midday, mid-afternoon, just after sunset and at night. Prayer, or *salah*, is one of the five pillars of Islam (see below).

The weekly *Id*

For most daily prayers Muslims do not have to go to the mosque. But on Fridays it is compulsory for men to go to the mosque for midday prayers. Women can choose whether to go. Going to the mosque on Friday is called *Jumu'ah* which means 'gathering'. At Friday prayers, Muslims also listen to a talk given by the **imam**, the person who leads the prayers. Friday is such a special occasion that it is called 'the weekly *Id*'.

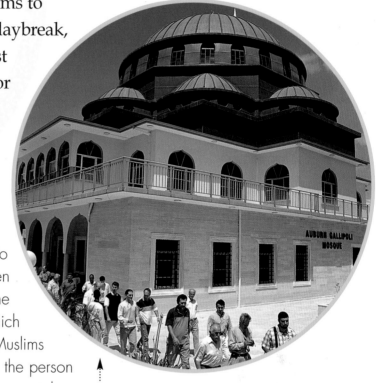

Muslims leaving the Gallipoli Mosque in Sydney, Australia, after Friday prayers.

The five pillars

The five pillars of Islam are five duties that Muslims perform. Just as real pillars support a building, these duties support the Islamic faith. The five pillars are:

1. The *Shahadah*, or declaration of faith. It says, 'There is no god but Allah, and Muhammad is the messenger of Allah.'

2. *Salah*, or prayer.

3. *Zakah*, or giving money to a worthy cause. All Muslims who can afford it must give a fixed amount each year.

4. *Sawm*, or fasting from daybreak to sunset during the month of *Ramadan* (see page 16).

5. *Hajj*, or pilgrimage to Makkah (see page 26).

The call to prayer

At five set times every day, the faithful are called to prayer. The call is made by a person called a *mu'adhin* from one of the mosque's minarets. Many mosques now have loudspeakers to help the *mu'adhin* to be heard. Before Muslims enter the mosque, they usually take off their shoes to help to keep the mosque clean. They must also wash before they pray. This is called **wudu**. They believe that this makes them fit and pure to talk to Allah.

This clock board shows the prayer times for each day. The dark clock shows the time for midday prayers on Friday.

Prayer positions

Prayers are said in Arabic and include verses from the Holy Qur'an. As Muslims pray they follow a set pattern of words and actions. This pattern is called a *rak'ah*. They stand upright as the prayer begins. Then they bow, kneel and touch the ground with their foreheads. A different part of the prayer is said with each of the actions.

Muslims pray with their whole bodies.

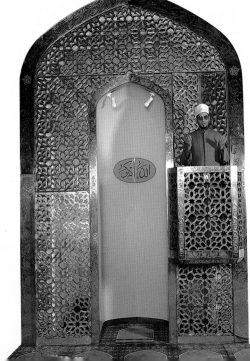

Every mosque has a qiblah *niche which shows the direction Muslims must face when praying. Muslims always pray facing towards the* **Ka'bah**, *the sacred building in Makkah's main mosque (see page 27).*

Al-Hijrah

The Muslim year starts with the month of *Muharram*. The first day of *Muharram* is New Year's Day, and is known as *Al-Hijrah* which means 'migration' or 'journey'. It marks the day, in 622CE, on which Muhammad was forced to leave Makkah and flee to the city of Madinah. The New Year is not officially celebrated in Islam but this date is so important that Muslims date their calendar from it. The letters 'AH' are written after Muslim dates to mean 'after/from the *Hijrah*'.

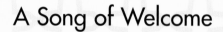

A Song of Welcome

This song was sung to welcome Muhammad to Madinah.

'The full Moon has risen.
We must be thankful
When a prophet calls us to Allah.
O Prophet, you have come with a call
Which we must obey.
You have come and honoured Madinah.
Welcome, O best of men.'

The journey to Madinah

In Makkah, Muhammad taught people about Allah. Many people followed him and became Muslims. But the powerful rulers of Makkah felt threatened by Muhammad and secretly plotted to kill him. Warned by the angel **Jibril**, Muhammad and his friend, Abu Bakr, escaped into the desert and made the long and difficult journey to safety in Madinah. There the Prophet was warmly welcomed and set up the first Muslim community.

◄ ················

The Prophet's Mosque in Madinah. The first mosque was built at Quba, on the outskirts of Madinah.

Ashura

On the tenth day of *Muharram*, known as *Ashura*, *Shi'ah* Muslims remember the death in 680CE of Husain, the grandson of Muhammad. The word 'Ashura' means 'ten'. In Husain's time the ruler of the Muslim world was a man called Yazid. But Husain refused to accept him as his leader. One day, Husain and his followers were travelling through the desert near Kerbala in Iraq. They were surrounded by Yazid's army who stopped them from reaching the river to drink. In the battle that followed, Husain was killed, along with many of his followers.

Husain's tomb in Kerbala, Iraq, has golden minarets.

This Shi'ah *Muslim is praying at a* **shrine** *of Husain.*

Sunni *and* Shi'ah

The two main groups of Muslims are *Sunni* and *Shi'ah*. About nine-tenths of Muslims are *Sunnis*. They follow the teachings of Muhammad and his chosen successors.

Shi'ah Muslims follow Husain's father, Ali, who was Muhammad's son-in-law, and his descendants. *Shi'ah* Muslims also follow Muhammad but they believe that Ali should have been chosen as his successor and so Islam was split into two groups.

Sunni Muslims do not mark Husain's death at *Ashura*. Instead, they follow Muhammad's example of fasting on this day and the day before.

Ashura processions

For *Shi'ah* Muslims, the first ten days of *Muharram* are a solemn time when they remember Husain's martyrdom. (A martyr is a person who is willing to die for their faith.) In India, *Shi'ah* Muslims dress in black clothes as a sign of mourning. The story of the Battle of Kerbala is acted out and verses recited in Husain's memory.

In Karachi, Pakistan, huge street processions take place, acting out the story of the Battle of Kerbala.

On Ashura, Shi'ah *Muslims pray at shrines that are replicas of Husain's tomb.*

On the day of Ashura itself, grand processions are held in the streets, with people carrying banners and elaborate replicas of Husain's tomb. The replicas are called *taziyas*. The marchers may be accompanied by brass bands and bagpipes playing sad tunes. Later, the *taziyas* are buried or thrown into the river. The processsion is led by a beautifully decorated white horse. Its empty saddle is a reminder of Husain's horse after its rider's death.

Free drinks

In some places, at *Ashura*, drinks such as water and fruit juice, are served to everyone free of charge. People say a prayer asking Allah to bless Husain as they drink. This reminds Muslims of how Yazid stopped Husain and his followers from reaching water.

Milad al-Nabi

In Arabic, the word 'milad' means 'birthday', and 'al-nabi' means 'the prophet'. *Milad al-Nabi* is Muhammad's birthday. It falls on the twelfth day of the month of *Rabi' al-Awwal*. Muhammad was born in Makkah in 570CE. He was orphaned at an early age and brought up first by his grandfather, then by his uncle. He grew up to be kind and hard-working, and was known as *al-Amin* which means 'the trustworthy one'. Muslims also remember Muhammad's death on the same day.

The *Sunnah*

The *Sunnah* is the name for the life of the Prophet Muhammad, and the example he set by what he did, said and approved. Muslims try to follow the *Sunnah* in the way they live their lives. They learn about Muhammad from books of *Seerah*, or biographies, and from the **Hadith**, which are collections of his sayings and teachings.

Birthday celebrations

Milad al-Nabi is a chance for Muslims to remember what Muhammad taught, and the lessons to be learnt from his life. Many Muslims mark the day by attending special meetings in the mosque. They listen to readings from the Holy Qur'an and stories about the Prophet's life. Some people invite their friends and family to a great feast. But some Muslims feel that it is wrong to celebrate this occasion because it was not marked by Muhammad nor by his closest companions.

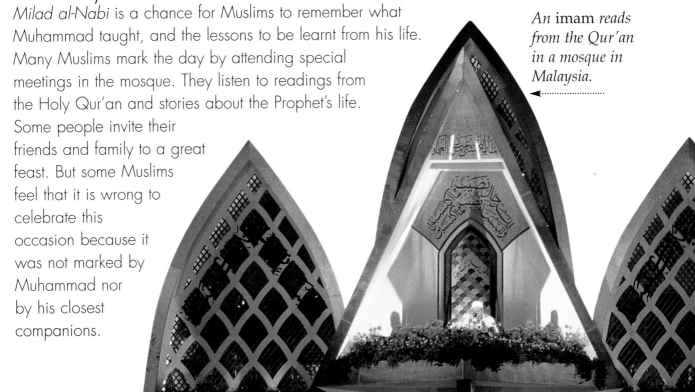

An imam reads from the Qur'an in a mosque in Malaysia.

Laylat-ul-Isra

The words 'Laylat-ul-Isra' mean 'the night of the journey'. This is a very special night for Muslims when they remember an amazing event in the life of the Prophet Muhammad.

The night of the journey

One night, the Prophet lay asleep in Makkah. The angel Jibril woke him up and took him on a journey to Jerusalem. There, Muhammad met the other prophets, including **Musa**, **Isa** and **Ibrahim**, and led them in prayer. Then Jibril led him up through the seven heavens into Allah's presence.

The Dome of the Rock, was built on the site in Jerusalem from which Muhammad is said to have ascended into heaven.

From the Holy Qur'an

This is how the Holy Qur'an describes the night of the journey:

'Exalted is Allah who took His servant [Muhammad] by night from the Sacred Mosque [in Makkah] to the Farthest Mosque [in Jerusalem], whose surroundings We have blessed.'

(The Qur'an, Chapter 17:1)

Praying

Allah gave Muhammad the command that all Muslims should pray 50 times a day. But Musa told Muhammad that people were too weak to say so many prayers. So Muhammad sent back to Allah and asked for the prayers to be reduced until only five prayers were left for each day. At that time, Muslims had to turn to face Jerusalem when they prayed. The direction of prayer was later changed to the *Ka'bah* in Makkah.

This Malaysian mosque has been lit up to celebrate Laylat-ul-Isra.

Marking the night journey

No one is sure of the date of the night journey but many Muslims mark it on the 27th day of *Rajab*. They try to spend this holy night in the mosque, praying, reading the Holy Qur'an and listening to talks. In some Muslim countries, houses, streets and mosques are decorated with colourful flags and lights. As with Muhammad's birthday, many Muslims recognise how important this event is but do not celebrate it.

Some Muslims stay up all night reading the Qur'an.

Ramadan

The ninth month of the Muslim year is called *Ramadan*. This is a very special time for all Muslims, wherever they live. During *Ramadan*, Muslims fast (go without food and drink) from daybreak until sunset. This fasting is called *sawm*, and is one of the five pillars of Islam. The instruction to fast at *Ramadan* is given in the Holy Qur'an.

A Muslim family shares a meal before dawn during Ramadan.

After sunset, many Muslim children like to break their fast with sweetmeats from the many street stalls.

Why Muslims fast

Ramadan is a special month for Muslims, because this is when Allah sent down the first words of the Holy Qur'an (see page 18). By fasting, Muslims show their thanks to Allah, learn self-discipline and experience what it is like to go hungry. This teaches them to appreciate how lucky they are to have enough to eat and drink the rest of the time. Fasting also brings the Muslim community together. Every adult Muslim is supposed to fast. But people who are old or sick, pregnant women, mothers with new-born babies, children under the age of seven, and travellers are excused.

A day in *Ramadan*

Ramadan is observed by all Muslims, although customs vary from country to country. After waking up early, Muslims eat a light breakfast before fasting begins at daybreak. Then they go to school, or get on with their work or daily chores, as usual. By sunset, everyone is hungry and thirsty. After the call to prayer, people break their fast with a sip of water and some dates, following the example set by Muhammad. They go to the mosque for prayers, then return home for their evening meal. Some large mosques provide a meal for poor or homeless people, or people who are alone.

Families watch as soldiers in Saudi Arabia prepare to fire the cannon to signal the start of the Ramadan *fast.*

Times of fasting

During *Ramadan*, the times of daybreak and sunset each day are published in the newspaper or broadcast on radio or television. These tell people when to begin and break their fast. The Holy Qur'an says that fasting must begin when there is enough light to tell the difference between a black thread and a white one. In some countries, people are woken up by a drummer, or the sound of a cannon being fired, to begin their fast.

Fasting can be difficult and uncomfortable, particularly in hot countries where many Muslims live. In Britain, during the long days of summer people may have to fast for 18 hours at a time. During winter though, the days, and the fast, are much shorter.

Laylat-ul-Qadr

A particularly holy time for Muslims is *Laylat-ul-Qadr*, or 'the night of power'. This is when they remember one of the greatest events in Islam – the first *revelation* of the Qur'an to the Prophet Muhammad. Muslims try to spend the night in the mosque, praying and reading the Holy Qur'an. By doing this, they hope to be granted the same number of blessings as if they prayed for a thousand months.

Often, when the Qur'an is read, it is placed on a stand to keep it clean and to show how important it is.

The cave on Mount Nur, the mountain of light, where Muhammad received the first revelation.

The first revelation

One night, in 610CE, when he was 40 years old, Muhammad was praying in a cave on Mount Nur, near Makkah. The angel Jibril appeared to him and ordered him to read. But Muhammad could not read or write. Three times, Jibril commanded him to read. Suddenly, Muhammad found that he understood. The words revealed to him that night were the first words of the Holy Qur'an (see opposite).

A night of worship

Muslims do not know the exact date of *Laylat-ul-Qadr*. All they know is that it falls on one of the last ten nights of *Ramadan*, on an odd-numbered night (21, 23, 25, 27, or 29). Some Muslims choose the 27th night of *Ramadan* because one of Muhammad's companions was sure that this was the correct night.

From the Holy Qur'an

These were the first words of the Holy Qur'an given to Muhammad:

'Read! in the name of your Lord who created, created people from drops of blood.
Read! and your Lord is the Most Generous, who taught by the pen, taught people what they did not know.'

(The Qur'an, Chapter 96: 1–5)

Islamic art

Muslims do not illustrate the Holy Qur'an with pictures of people. They believe that Allah alone creates people, not human artists. Instead, they use beautiful writing, called **calligraphy**, and elaborate patterns.

Try decorating a page with geometric shapes and flowers. Then write the *Bismillah* in Arabic. These words begin most of the chapters of the Holy Qur'an, and mean 'In the name of Allah, the compassionate, the merciful'.

Reading the Holy Qur'an

Muslims believe that the Holy Qur'an is the word of Allah. They use it as a guide for their lives and treat it with great respect. Muslims wash before touching or reading the Holy Qur'an, to make them clean and pure. When a copy is not in use, it is placed on a high shelf and covered with a clean cloth. No other books may be placed on top of it.

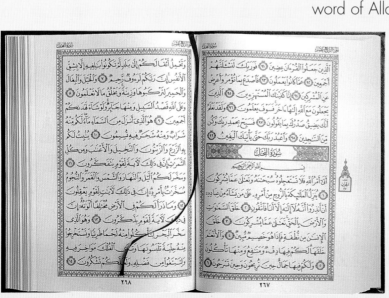

◀ *Everything that Allah told to the Prophet Muhammad is written in the Qur'an.*

Id-ul-Fitr

The great festival of *Id-ul-Fitr* marks the breaking of the fast at the end of *Ramadan*. ('Fitr' means 'breaking fast'.) It starts when the new moon is seen in the night sky, which shows that the month of *Shawwal* has begun.

Id is a popular time for family outings. These people are visiting the sacred carp pool at Seker Bayram in Turkey.

In Nigeria, Id-ul-Fitr *is often celebrated with fairs.*

Muslims meeting for communal prayers in a park in Washington, USA.

The festival of *Id*

The festival lasts for one day, although in some countries Muslims set aside two or three more days as a holiday. *Id-ul-Fitr* is sometimes called 'Lesser *Id*'. The festival of *Id-ul-Adha* (see page 24) is known as 'Greater *Id*' because it has more religious importance. *Id-ul-Fitr* is a very happy occasion for Muslims everywhere. It is a chance for them to come together to celebrate their faith. It is also a time for forgiving people for the things they have done wrong.

Giving to charity

Before *Id* begins, all Muslims who can afford it must make a special gift of money to charity. This payment is called *zakat-ul-Fitr*, (the 'payment of breaking fast'). The amount each person must give is the price of a meal. This is given to Muslims who are poor and needy so that they are remembered on this day and can afford to join in with the *Id* celebrations. It can be given directly to those who need it, or collected by the mosque to be shared out.

Thousands of people attend dawn prayers at Id *at the Mahmoud Mosque in Cairo, Egypt.*

Prayers for *Id*

On *Id* morning, everyone gets up early, bathes and puts on their best clothes. These are often new clothes, specially bought for *Id*. Then people go to *Id* prayers, to thank Allah for sending the Holy Qur'an and for making them strong enough to fast during *Ramadan*. There is always a huge crowd for *Id* prayers. If the weather is good, prayers may be said outside in a large field or a park. Otherwise, prayers take place inside the mosque. Afterwards, the *imam* gives a talk about the meaning of the *Id* festival. Then the people wish each other '*Id Mubarak*', which means 'Happy *Id*', and hug or shake hands.

An *Id* Prayer

'Allah is great, Allah is great,
Allah is great.
There is no god but Allah.
Allah is great, Allah is great,
To Him all praise belongs.
Allah is the greatest,
All praise is due to Him.
And glory to Allah,
In the evening and
the morning,
There is no god but Allah
the Unique.'

Celebrating
Id-ul-Fitr

When prayers are over, families get together to celebrate *Id* at home. In some Muslim countries people have a few days' holiday from school and work. This is a time for visiting friends and relations. There are parties and presents for children, who also receive *Id* pocket money. A delicious *Id* feast is prepared. The type of food cooked depends on where people live. In India, a delicious, sweet pudding made of fine noodles is very popular. In some Muslim countries there are colourful parades, funfairs and even camel-racing.

A Malaysian family sharing a feast during Id.

An *Id* card

Many Muslims exchange special greetings cards at *Id*.

Try designing your own Id *card:*

1. Fold a piece of card in half.

2. Decorate the front with a picture of a mosque, stars and the new moon.

3. Write '*Id Mubarak*', or 'Happy *Id*', inside.

For more ideas about making *Id* cards, look on the internet (see page 30).

Id-ul-Adha

The second great festival of the Muslim year is *Id-ul-Adha*. (The Arabic word 'Adha' means 'sacrifice'.) It is known as 'Greater *Id*' because it is a more important religious festival than *Id-ul-Fitr*. The festival lasts for four days in the month of *Dhul-Hijjah*, at the end of the Hajj (see page 26).

To celebrate Id-ul-Adha, *many people buy biscuits and sweetmeats at street stalls.*

The festival of sacrifice

At *Id-ul-Adha*, Muslims remember the story of the Prophet Ibrahim which is told in the Qur'an. Ibrahim dreamt that Allah wanted him to kill his beloved son, Ismail. To show his willingness to obey Allah, Ibrahim got ready to kill Ismail. Then Ibrahim heard Allah's voice, telling him to stop. Allah told Ibrahim that he had proved his love by being willing to give up his precious son. He gave Ibrahim a ram to sacrifice instead. This was the beginning of *Id-ul-Adha*, the festival of sacrifice.

Celebrating *Id-ul-Adha*

Like *Id-ul-Fitr*, *Id-ul-Adha* is a very happy time for Muslims all over the world. Many of the ways of celebrating are similar. Early in the morning, Muslims dress in their best clothes and set off to the mosque for *Id* prayers. They listen to a talk by the *imam* about the importance of *Hajj*. To remind people of Ibrahim's sacrifice, a sheep or goat, or sometimes a camel, is killed. Prayers are said for the animal so that its life is given to Allah. Some of the meat is shared out among friends and family. Some is given to the poor, so that they can join in the *Id* feast. People also exchange *Id* cards, and gifts of sweets.

*In many mosques, the **imam** gives out sweets to children.*

Hand decorations

At festival times, Muslim girls and women often paint their hands with beautiful patterns, drawn in reddish-orange *mehndi*, or henna dye. If you want to be able to wash off the patterns easily, try using body paints instead of henna paste.

To decorate your hands:

1. Mix some henna powder with a few drops of oil, to make a thick paste.

2. Dab your hand with lemon juice. This will make the henna stick.

3. Use a matchstick to draw a pattern on your hand with the henna paste.

4. Leave the paste to dry, then scrape it off carefully. The pattern will last for about a week.

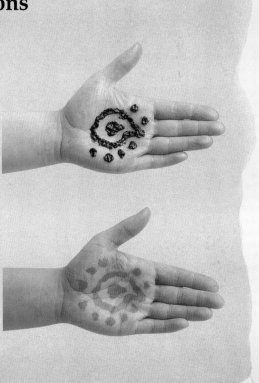

The Hajj

Dhul-Hijjah is the month of the annual *Hajj* pilgrimage to Makkah. *Hajj* is one of the five pillars of Islam, and all Muslims try to make the pilgrimage at least once in their lifetimes.

The pilgrimage

When they arrive in Makkah, pilgrims walk seven times around the *Ka'bah*, the sacred building at the heart of Makkah's main mosque.

Then they walk or run between two nearby hills, to remember the story of Hajar (the wife of the Prophet Ibrahim) who ran looking for water for her baby son.

Next, the pilgrims go to the Plain of Arafat where Muhammad preached his last sermon. They stand for a whole afternoon in the hot sun, where they pray and beg forgiveness for their sins, before camping overnight at Muzdalifah.

The next day, at a place called Mina, they throw stones at three pillars which stand for the Devil. The Devil tried to tempt Ismail to disobey his father. Finally, the pilgrims return to Makkah and walk around the *Ka'bah* seven more times.

Millions of Muslims follow this route each year for Hajj. *Being together teaches them to feel part of the Muslim community and to look after their neighbours.*

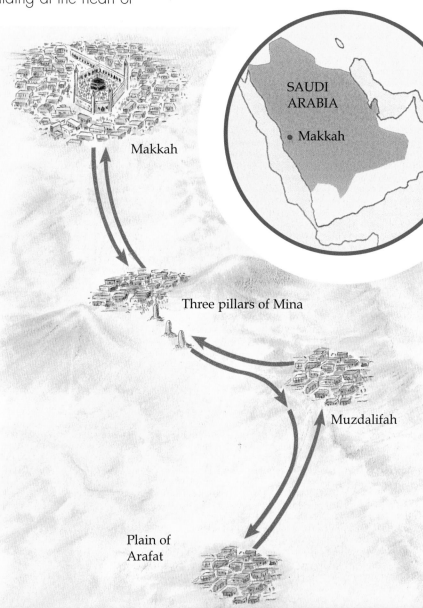

Makkah

SAUDI ARABIA

• Makkah

Three pillars of Mina

Muzdalifah

Plain of Arafat

Hajj clothes

During *Hajj* pilgrims wear special clothes called **Ihram**. All the men dress identically, in two plain white cotton sheets wrapped around their bodies. This shows that everyone, rich and poor, is the same in Allah's eyes. There are no set clothes for women. They wear their normal, modest clothes.

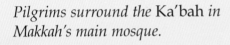

Pilgrims surround the Ka'bah *in Makkah's main mosque.*

The *Ka'bah*

Muslims believe that the *Ka'bah* was originally built by **Adam**, then later rebuilt by Ibrahim and his son Ismail. As they were working on it, they were given a black stone by the angel Jibril, which they built into one corner. Pilgrims try to touch or kiss the stone as they walk round the *Ka'bah*.

A model of the cube-shaped Ka'bah.

Festival Calendar

Date	Islamic month	Festival
1	Muharram	Al-Hijrah
10	Muharram	Ashura
12	Rabi' al-Awwal	Milad al-Nabi
27	Rajab	Laylat-ul-Isra
	Ramadan	Ramadan
21, 23, 25, 27 or 29	Ramadan	Laylat-ul-Qadr
1	Shawwal	Id-ul-Fitr
8–13	Dhul-Hijjah	The Hajj
10–13	Dhul-Hijjah	Id-ul-Adha

Islamic months

The 12 months of the Islamic year are called:

1	Muharram
2	Safar
3	Rabi' al-Awwal
4	Rabi' al-Thani
5	Jumada al-Awwal
6	Jumada al-Thani
7	Rajab
8	Sha'ban
9	Ramadan
10	Shawwal
11	Dhul-Qa'dah
12	Dhul-Hijjah

Note:

The Islamic calendar is based on the moon and has a shorter year than the standard Western calendar. This means it is impossible to give equivalent dates for festivals in the everyday calendar, as they fall at different times each year.

Glossary

Adam	For Muslims, the first man and the first prophet of Allah.
Arabic	The language in which the Holy Qur'an is written and the sacred language of Islam.
Bismillah	The words 'In the name of Allah' which begin every verse of the Holy Qur'an, except the ninth.
Calligraphy	A beautiful type of writing used for decoration.
Hadith	The sayings of the Prophet Muhammad.
Hajj	The annual pilgrimage to Makkah which all Muslims must try to make at least once in their lives.
Holy Qur'an	The sacred book of the Muslims.
Ibrahim	A prophet of Islam. He is also known as Abraham and is important for Jews and Christians.
Ihram	The plain white clothes worn by male pilgrims on the *Hajj*.
Imam	A Muslim who leads prayers in the mosque.
Isa	A prophet of Islam. In Christianity, he is known as Jesus.
Jibril	The angel who revealed the words of the Holy Qur'an to Muhammad. He is also known as Gabriel.
Ka'bah	A cube-shaped building in Makkah. Muslims turn to face the *Ka'bah* when they pray.
Minaret	The tower on or near a mosque that is used to call Muslims to prayer.
Mosque	A building where Muslims meet and worship.
Mu'adhin	The person who calls Muslims to prayer.
Musa	A prophet of Islam. He is also known as Moses and is important for Jews and Christians.
Prophet	A person chosen by Allah to be his messenger.
Rak'ah	A unit of *salah*, or prayer. It is made up of a pattern of set movements and verses.
Revelation	An experience in which an important teaching is revealed, or made clear.
Salah	Muslim prayers. Muslims must pray five time a day, as taught by the Prophet Muhammad.
Shi'ah	Muslims who believe that Ali and his descendants were the rightful leaders of Islam after Muhammad.
Shrine	A place of worship linked with a sacred person or object.
Sunnah	The thoughts, actions and examples of the Prophet Muhammad which are followed by Muslims.
Sunni	Muslims who believe that Muhammad's close companions were Muhammad's rightful successors.
Wudu	The practice of washing before entering a mosque or reading the Holy Qur'an.
Zakat-ul-Fitr	A payment made to charity at the end of *Ramadan*.

Further Resources

Books

A World of Festivals: Ramadan and Id-ul-Fitr
Rosalind Kerven, Evans Brothers 1997

Celebrations! Ramadan and Id-ul-Fitr
Mandy Ross, Heinemann 2001

Celebration!
Barnabas and Annabel Kindersley,
Dorling Kindersley 1997

Festivals in World Religions
The Shap Working Party on World Religions
in Education 1998

What do we know about Islam?
Shahrukh Husain, Hodder Wayland 1996

Beliefs and Cultures: Muslim
Richard Tames, Franklin Watts 1996

Websites

www.festivals.com
Information about festivals, holy days and
holidays.

www.muslim-ed-trust.org.uk
The website of the Muslim Educational Trust.
It advises and produces a wide range of
materials on Islam.

www.eidmubarak.com
A selection of greetings cards for Id.

www.unn.ac.uk/societies/islamic
Information about Islamic beliefs, history and
civilisation.

www.islam-australia.iinet.net.au
Information about Muslims in Australia.

Index